Meditations
for the heart

—

HEART QUESTIONS
FOR ALL OF LIFE

KRISTIN SCHMUCKER
& SARAH MORRISON

MEDITATIONS
1
FOR THE HEART

♥

WHAT AM I DOING TODAY THAT MATTERS FOR ETERNITY?

—

Because of Jesus Christ, Christians have an eternal hope.

We have hope because this world is not forever, sin will one day be abolished, and tears will be wiped away by our heavenly Father. Our hope doesn't reside in anything this world offers us—our hope resides in Christ. We know that this world and all that is within it will one day pass away, and we will be ushered into the new heaven and new earth where we will live with God and be His people. This eternal focus shifts the way that we behave on earth. Our minds ought to be set on things above; we are called to dwell on God and things that are aligned with Him. Because of our hope in eternity, we are compelled in our sanctification, gospel-stewardship, and an ever-growing affection for God.

Scripture to meditate on:

+ Psalm 39:4-5
+ Romans 12:1
+ Ephesians 2:10

+ Philippians 4:8
+ Hebrews 6:10

our hope resides in Christ

Who can I encourage today?

How can I share the gospel today?

How am I feeding my own soul with eternal things today?

MEDITATIONS
2
FOR THE HEART

WHAT BRINGS YOU THE MOST JOY IN YOUR LIFE?

—

Some things might expand joy, others might steal joy; nevertheless, we spend our days pining after joy. Things like a good meal, a beautiful song, or a good book might bring us joy, but we find that those things bring only temporal joy. In Scripture, we find that as believers we can find joy in suffering, joy in worship, and joy in faith. But in all of those things, that joy is rooted in the joy of the Lord. We can feel the tension between the joy we find in the Lord and the joy found enjoying the things He's given us on earth. In that way, the source of our joy can be a litmus test for where the affection of our heart is, and we may find that we are living for temporal joy from the things He has given to us rather than for the Lord—the source of all joy.

Scripture to meditate on:

+ Psalm 4:7   + James 1:2-31

+ Psalm 30:5   + Peter 1:8-9

+ Hebrews 12:2

How would you define joy?

What does your source of joy reflect about your spiritual life?

How can you practically seek to find more joy in the Lord and His purposes?

MEDITATIONS
3
FOR THE HEART

♥

WHAT GIVES YOU
SECURITY?

—

Each of us is liable to seek security in earthly things.

Whether it be money, relationships, family, or a tightly-held future, we can grip these things with white knuckles and rely on them for our hope and safety. But that's not the gospel, and that's not our true hope. We rest and rely on Jesus Christ's sacrifice to make us whole and holy, and we find security in the future He has for us. This future isn't one of brick and mortar on this earth though. Our sense of security as Christians is eternal, imperishable, and everlasting. If we are in Christ, we have a hope of dwelling alongside the Lord, we have a future that will not be taken from us, and we have a security in being held and loved by God.

Scripture to meditate on:

+ Deuteronomy 33:27
+ Isaiah 54:17

+ John 10:28-29
+ 2 Timothy 1:12

we find security in the future He has for us

Are the things that you seek security in temporal or eternal?

What are practical ways that you can shift your sense of security to God?

What testimony does it give to a watching world if you choose security in God over money, family, or other sources?

MEDITATIONS
4
FOR THE HEART

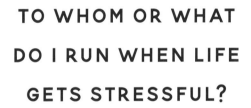

TO WHOM OR WHAT DO I RUN WHEN LIFE GETS STRESSFUL?

—

LIFE IS SURE TO GET STRESSFUL AT ONE TIME OR ANOTHER.

Perhaps you are stressed about work, or family, or illness, or maybe you're putting a lot of pressure on yourself this season. Whatever the case may be, what we run to reveals our biggest comforts. Are we comforted in God or in food? Are we comforted in Scripture or in exercise? What do we rely on to heal us and make us feel better, and do those things actually do the trick? As believers, we have a sturdy hope in the Lord. When we run to His Word, we know that we are being fed the truth, and we are given vitality through that truth. Our stressors may not disappear, but the Lord is more powerful than the stress that we experience on this earth.

Scripture to meditate on:

+ Psalm 55:22

+ 2 Corinthians 4:7-9

+ 2 Corinthians 12:9

+ 2 Thessalonians 3:16

+ James 1:2-4

16

Do the people or things you run to when stressed actually solve the problem?

In what ways does stress impact your relationship with God?

How can we use stress to strengthen our faith?

MEDITATIONS
FOR THE HEART
5

AM I JUSTIFYING
SIN IN MY LIFE?

—

We all know that we are not sinless.

The only One who was able to flee the temptation of sin and live perfectly is Jesus Christ. It can be difficult and even frustrating that we are still creatures who are prone to sin even though we've been made new in Jesus. The battle against sin is not yet over though. We must wage war against our sinful patterns each day of our lives. It is important to realize that unrepentant sin affects our relationship with God and others, and repentance and confession are crucial tenants of the Christian life. However, we are unable to partake in such tenants if we refuse to critically self-reflect. We must consistently ask for the Holy Spirit to reveal our sinful ways, strengthening us to turn from them.

Scripture to meditate on:

+ 1 Corinthians 10:13
+ Galatians 5:19-21
+ James 4:17
+ James 4:7
+ 1 John 1:9

we must wage war against our sinful patterns each day

How is sin impacting my spiritual life? How does my sin impact those around me?

What practical safeguards can I put in place to ward off temptation?

Do I know my limits? How can I make the decision to flee from sin in a world that encourages it?

MEDITATIONS
6
FOR THE HEART

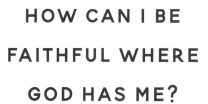

HOW CAN I BE FAITHFUL WHERE GOD HAS ME?

—

23

WHERE WE ARE NOW IS NOT ALWAYS WHERE WE WANT TO BE.

As the saying goes, the grass always looks greener on the other side. However, no matter how hard we wish, sometimes our circumstances do not change. Sometimes that new job doesn't come through, or the house doesn't sell, or the season's just not quite over. How we respond in those situations reveals to us where our hope and contentment are found. When we ask ourselves how we can remain faithful amid the "right now" circumstances we're in, we're submitting to God's sovereignty and humbling ourselves before His plan.

Scripture to meditate on:

+ Matthew 25:21

+ Romans 12:11-12

+ 2 Timothy 4:6-8

+ Hebrews 11:1-2

+ Hebrews 12:1-2

What does it mean to be faithful?

Why does God have you in this place or season?
How can you use this time to grow spiritually?

Can I be truly faithful to God if my heels are dug into
the ground and my fists are clenched?

MEDITATIONS
7
FOR THE HEART

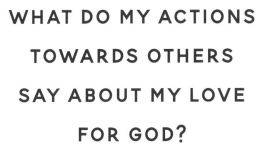

WHAT DO MY ACTIONS TOWARDS OTHERS SAY ABOUT MY LOVE FOR GOD?

—

Whether we realize it or not, others are always watching us.

When we are driving in our cars, interacting on social media, or conducting our lives at the grocery store, our love for God is on display. We can speak of our love for the Lord, but if our actions don't match, we're just making noise. The selfless, incredible love that Christ displayed on the cross ought to pour into us daily, so much so that it pours out onto others. If our love for our neighbors isn't apparent, we must reflect on why that might be the case. Can others see God's love in our behavior?

Scripture to meditate on:

+ Matthew 5:43-48
+ 1 Corinthians 13:1
+ Philippians 2:3-4
+ 1 John 4:7-8
+ 1 John 4:19-21

if our actions don't match, we're just making noise

Who can I love today? How can I intentionally care for others today?

How can my acts of love toward neighbors reflect and testify to the love of Christ?

Do I find it difficult to love others? Why or why not?

MEDITATIONS
8
FOR THE HEART

HOW WOULD THE KINGDOM OF GOD GROW IF I LEVERAGED MY GIFTS AND RESOURCES?

—

EVERY SINGLE ONE OF US HAS GIFTS AND RESOURCES.

Not one of those gifts or resources is small in the eyes of the Lord who has gifted them to us. Whether we have talent, or money, or time, or anything else, we would do well to meditate on how to leverage those things for the Lord. If we squander our gifts and resources, we neglect the purposes of the Giver. But if we should leverage these things, giving them back to the Lord as a sacrifice, the Kingdom of God is edified and built up. When we look indiscriminately at what the Lord has entrusted us with, we have an opportunity to give those gifts back to God in praise.

Scripture to meditate on:

+ Exodus 35:10

+ Matthew 6:1-4

+ 1 Corinthians 12:5-6

+ Ephesians 2:10

+ 1 Peter 4:10-11

What talents, gifts, or resources do I have? What are practical ways I can use them?

Do I have a tendency to hoard my time, money, or talents for my own benefit or do I use them for the church?

What would it take for me to view my time as a resource and leverage it for the gospel?

MEDITATIONS
FOR THE HEART
9

DO I STEWARD
MY SUFFERING?

—

Suffering comes in all shapes and sizes.

No matter the size, the pain still remains. Our inclinations might be to avoid suffering, to speed on past it, or to linger there. But what happens when we look at our suffering in the eye and recognize that God can use it? In stewarding our sufferings, we are invited into Christlikeness after Jesus who suffered in every way as we do yet remained without sin. When suffering comes—and it will come—we have the option to yield ourselves to it, asking God to transform us with it. The real question is not whether we will suffer or what will cause suffering for us. Instead, it's asking if we're willing to let God use the suffering we encounter for our good and His glory.

Scripture to meditate on:

+ Psalm 119:71   + 2 Corinthians 4:17

+ Luke 14:27   + Philippians 3:10

+ Romans 5:3-4

for our good and His glory

How would my life change if I used suffering to bring me closer to God?

How would my view of suffering change if I saw it as an opportunity for sanctification?

How will others be drawn to Christ if I choose to cling to God amid suffering?

MEDITATIONS
10
FOR THE HEART

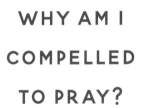

WHY AM I COMPELLED TO PRAY?

—

PRAYER IS AN IMPORTANT PART OF THE CHRISTIAN'S LIFE.

Without a second thought, we often incorporate prayer into mealtimes and before bed, but why else should we pray? Prayer is our communication line to God in all things—needs, praises, reflections, prayers for ourselves, and prayers for others. It is important for us to reflect on how we view prayer, and if that lines up with Scripture. Through prayer, do we find ourselves using God or is it merely another task to check off in our daily routine? When we approach God with a posture that is delighting in Him, eager for His presence, and humbled to His purposes, our prayer time is bolstered and strengthened. So, do we use prayer as a tool or do we view it as a crucial part of our relationship with God?

Scripture to meditate on:

+ Matthew 6:9-13

+ Luke 6:12

+ Luke 18:1-8

+ James 5:13

Are my prayers mostly consisting of praise, requests, or needs?

How would the world change if all my prayers were answered?

How can I improve my prayer life?

MEDITATIONS
11
FOR THE HEART

♥

WHAT LIES HAVE I ALLOWED TO WARP MY THOUGHTS AND ACTIONS?

—

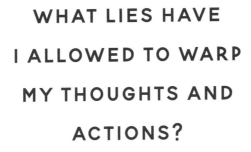

Every day we're fed lies from our televisions, from social media, and sometimes from friends and family.

Too often, our society and culture don't base what they present on the truth of God's Word. They instead focus on what benefits the individual. As Christians, we have to be diligent to discern what is the truth, measuring what we hear and see against Scripture. Daily we're assaulted with lies about our identity, our worth, our needs, and what is right for us. If we fail to measure these assertions against the rubric of Scripture, we will certainly fall into traps and snares.

Scripture to meditate on:

+ Proverbs 3:5-6
+ 2 Corinthians 10:5
+ Galatians 5:7-9
+ Colossians 2:8
+ 1 Timothy 6:3

measuring what we hear and see against Scripture

How have the lies I have believed affected my walk with God?

What are the practical ways I can combat the lies of the world?

How can my propensity to believe lies impact my prayer life?

MEDITATIONS
12
FOR THE HEART

♥

HOW WOULD THE KINGDOM OF GOD BE IMPACTED IF ALL MY PRAYERS WERE ANSWERED?

—

Each of us has needs and worries that we request to God, and it is a good thing to bring those things before the Lord. But what about our churches, our families, the mission field, and our cities—would these things be impacted if our prayers were all answered? It's important to reflect on these things, asking ourselves if God's kingdom would be advanced if our prayers were answered. When we reflect on these matters, we're confronted with whether or not we actually care about things that have an eternal impact.

Scripture to meditate on:

+ 2 Chronicles 7:14

+ Matthew 5:44

+ Matthew 6:9-13

+ Ephesians 6:18

+ 1 Timothy 2:1-2

+ 1 John 5:14-15

Are my concerns God's concerns?

If all my prayers were answered, would people be saved?
Disciples formed? Sin overcome? The great commission
advanced?

How can I practically incorporate broader prayers along
with my personal prayers?

MEDITATIONS
13
FOR THE HEART

WHAT IS DISTRACTING ME FROM GOD'S MISSION?

—

Within moments of waking up, we have the ability to get distracted.

Maybe we're distracted by our phones, our finances, or what lies ahead of us for that day. In any case, distractions are endless, and they can be big or small. The question is less about if these distractions exist and more about how to abstain and refrain from the distractions that are surely around. If we place our energy that is currently given to distractions toward the purposes of God, how might our spiritual lives be transformed? How might our lives look different?

Scripture to meditate on:

+ Matthew 28:18-20
+ Matthew 24:14
+ Acts 1:8
+ Acts 2:24-47
+ 1 Peter 2:9-10

place our energy toward the purposes of God

Do I leverage things like money, time, and technology for the kingdom, or do I allow these things to distract me?

How can I actively participate in God's work and His will?

In what ways would my life change if I limited or eradicated my distractions?

MEDITATIONS
14
FOR THE HEART

WHO CAN I ENCOURAGE AND POINT TO THE LORD?

—

WE ARE MEMBERS OF CHRIST'S CHURCH, AND OUR SPIRITUAL FAMILY OFTEN NEEDS ENCOURAGEMENT.

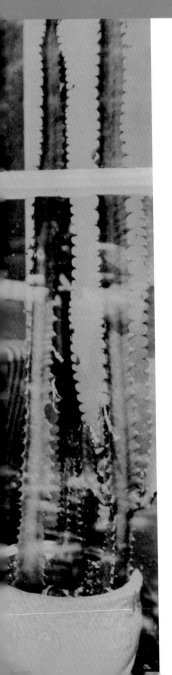

When we encourage others, we empower and embolden them toward the things of God. There are countless times and ways in which we can encourage others. Maybe that means encouraging them in their study of the Bible, encouraging them to use their giftings for the glory of God, or encouraging them when sorrows and suffering are deep. Whatever the case may be, there are plenty of individuals around you that you can and should be encouraging, pointing them to the Lord.

Scripture to meditate on:

+ John 15:12

+ Romans 15:1

+ Galatians 6:2

+ Philippians 2:3-4

+ Hebrews 6:10

What is stopping me from encouraging, caring for, and loving my neighbors?

Am I withholding anything (tangible or emotional) from those in need around me?

What does my giving or withholding express about Jesus Christ?

MEDITATIONS
15
FOR THE HEART

♥

WHO IS MARGINALIZED OR NEEDY IN MY CONTEXT, AND HOW CAN I HELP POINT THEM TO CHRIST?

—

Needs persist all around us.

Financial needs, social needs, and support needs are all common examples. Whether you focus on those in your neighborhood, your church, or in your city at large, there's no shortage of those who are in great physical need and great spiritual need. When we consider these neighbors' needs as higher than our own, how might our communities be changed? If we leverage the little or plenty of what we have, how might the meeting of a physical need point the individuals towards their spiritual need in Christ Jesus? By practicing empathy, compassion, and sensitivity to who God has placed in our lives, our communities could be radically changed.

Scripture to meditate on:

+ Jeremiah 22:3

+ 1 Corinthians 10:24

+ Luke 4:18-19

+ James 2:15-16

+ Romans 12:13

+ 1 John 3:17

there's no shortage of those in physical and spiritual need

How would the world change if Christians within their local contexts cared for the physical needs of their community?

What role does empathy play in sharing the gospel?

Who has God placed in my life to care for?

MEDITATIONS
16
FOR THE HEART

♥

DO I VALUE
ACCOUNTABILITY
IN MY LIFE?

And none of us can go through life slaying sin on our own. We have a deep need for the Holy Spirit's guidance, for the Son's advocacy, and for the Father's mercy. Part of the Christian life that can easily be ignored is the act of confession. When we have mature believers in our lives, they become an indispensable resource to us. Submitting to others in allowing ourselves to be vulnerable about the sins with which we struggle can be transformative in our spiritual lives. Having fellowship with other believers with whom we can be held accountable is crucial to our growth.

Scripture to meditate on:

+ Proverbs 27:17

+ 2 Corinthians 5:10

+ Galatians 6:1-5

+ James 4:17

+ James 5:16

+ For further thought

How can I move forward in God's strength?

_____

_____

_____

_____

_____

Is there sin I need to confess or an attitude I need
to change?

_____

_____

_____

_____

_____

Do I have enough confidence in the sufficiency of
Christ's sacrifice to be emboldened to confess sin and
be held accountable?

_____

_____

_____

_____

_____

_____

♥

IS MY TONGUE
DISCIPLINED?

—

Our tongues are the most powerful muscle in our bodies.

They are able to give life or bring about death by the mere words that they form. For the Christian, our tongues can cause ourselves or others to stumble; they can fester in sin should we refuse to train and tame our tongues. They can share the gospel, or they can participate in gossip. They can encourage, or they can tear down. If we aren't careful, our tongues can bring destruction. Therefore it is important to consider: is your tongue being used properly? Are you speaking of things that are good, lovely, wise, and true?

Scripture to meditate on:

+ Proverbs 15:4

+ Matthew 12:36

+ Ephesians 4:29

+ James 3:5-12

speak what is good, lovely, wise, and true

In what ways have I let my tongue go unchecked?

How can my tongue lead myself and others to the Lord?

If I were to read a manuscript of every word I've spoken in the last week, would I be pleased or disgusted?

MEDITATIONS
18
FOR THE HEART

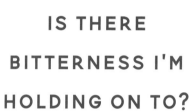

IS THERE BITTERNESS I'M HOLDING ON TO?

—

BITTERNESS IS SOMETHING WE CAN CLING TO LIKE NOTHING ELSE.

Often, we find ourselves holding on to hurts more than we rely on forgiveness. But forgiveness is the biggest companion of our faith; for by it, we are offered life in Jesus Christ. When we experience the scandalous love of Christ, we are offered the opportunity to relinquish the bitterness that we hold on to and instead grasp on to love and forgiveness. Whether our bitterness is aimed at others or our circumstances, in Christ, we have the opportunity and obligation to let go of it, and instead embrace the contentment and freedom waiting for us in God.

Scripture to meditate on:

+ Mark 11:25

+ 1 Corinthians 13:4-7

+ Ephesians 4:31-32

+ Hebrews 12:15

+ For further thought

What does my bitterness imply about Christ's love?
Is it an accurate reflection?

Is there anyone I need to forgive right now?

How can letting go of bitterness strengthen my
relationship with God?

MEDITATIONS
19
FOR THE HEART

♥

WHAT HOLDS FIRST PLACE IN MY HEART RIGHT NOW?

—

Where do our affections land?

In our society, we are permitted to allow our affections for family, friends, dreams, and desires to take up space in our hearts, forcing out our affection for God. We tend to look to earthly things to make us content or feel at ease, yet as Christians, we know that this will not last. We must look to the imperishable nature of God and our future with Him to truly be secure, at ease, and content. The only lasting contentment and joy are found in God. We allow ourselves to become distracted, not seeing God for who He truly is. And in so doing, we jeopardize our affections, allowing earthly things to creep in and steal the place in our heart that rightfully belongs to the Lord alone.

Scripture to meditate on:

+ Deuteronomy 6:5
+ Judges 10:14
+ Jonah 2:8
+ Colossians 3:5
+ 1 John 5:21

we must look to the imperishable nature of God

What idols seek to steal your affections from God?

What role do emotions play in seeking God first?

How can we guard our affections of the Lord?

MEDITATIONS
20
FOR THE HEART

♥

WHAT ARE YOUR
GOALS OR DREAMS?

—

It is important to consider if these goals and dreams include or exclude God. Are we operating according to our own selfish desires for glory, or are we working with kingdom-mindedness in our hearts? Are we allowing ourselves to be used by God, or are we running from His intended purposes for us? When we consider and submit ourselves to the work that God has intended, we are prompted to meditate on our own ambitions. Do each of these things align? We honor God when we submit toward His intended purpose, and we honor Him in humility when we work diligently to meet those goals.

Scripture to meditate on:

+ Psalm 127:1

+ Proverbs 3:6

+ Proverbs 16:3, 9

+ Romans 12:2

+ Philippians 3:13-14

What do your goals or dreams reveal about your heart?

Are your hands open before God, willing to accept
His plans?

How can your goal-centered work be a reflection of
the gospel?

May the words of my mouth and the meditation of my heart be acceptable to you, Lord, my rock and my Redeemer.

PSALM 19:14

Thank You

for studying God's Word with us

CONNECT WITH US

@THEDAILYGRACECO
@KRISTINSCHMUCKER

CONTACT US

INFO@THEDAILYGRACECO.COM

SHARE

#THEDAILYGRACECO
#LAMPANDLIGHT

VISIT US ONLINE

THEDAILYGRACECO.COM

MORE DAILY GRACE!

THE DAILY GRACE APP
DAILY GRACE PODCAST